SO-BZU-025

DISNEY'S
THE EMPEROR'S
NEW GROOVE
Joke Book

REBECCA GÓMEZ

DISNEY
PRESS

NEW YORK

Copyright © 2000 by Disney Enterprises, Inc. All rights reserved.
No part of this book may be reproduced or transmitted in any form
or by any means, electronic or mechanical, including photocopying,
recording, or by any information storage and retrieval system,
without written permission from the publisher.
For more information address Disney Press, 114 Fifth Avenue,
New York, New York 10011-5690.
Printed in the United States of America
First Edition

10 9 8 7 6 5 4 3 2 1

ISBN: 0-7868-4428-0

Library of Congress Catalog Card Number: 00-101749

For more Disney Press fun, visit www.disneybooks.com

What do you get when you
cross Kuzco with a llama?

A very hairy emperor!

Why doesn't Kronk like ice fishing?
**Because the
cubes are too small!**

Why did Kronk's parents
name him Kronk?
**Because "Dumb"
was already taken!**

Why did Kronk have to
go back to the doctor?
**Because he failed
the blood test!**

Why did Kronk
cross the road?
**Duh . . .
he forgot!**

YZMA:
"I want to picnic here, Kronk. Shoo the flies."
KRONK:
"Aw, Yzma, can't we
let them go barefoot?"

Why did Kronk hang
Popsicles on his shirt?
Because Yzma
said she needed
an ice chest!

How does Kronk climb trees?
He sits on seeds
and waits!

KNOCK, KNOCK.
Who's there?
Elise.
Elise, who?
**Elise you're not
stuck in the jungle
with Kuzco!**

KNOCK, KNOCK.
Who's there?
Ben.
Ben, who?
Ben a llama lately?

KNOCK, KNOCK.
Who's there?
Canoe.
Canoe, who?
**Canoe help Pacha
herd llamas?**

6

KNOCK, KNOCK.
Who's there?
Ima.
Ima, who?
**Ima going to ask Yzma
to turn Kuzco into a fish!**

KNOCK, KNOCK.
Who's there?
Ida.
Ida, who?
**Ida let Kronk
cook dinner!**

KNOCK, KNOCK.
Who's there?
Hope.
Hope, who?
**Hope Kuzco
finds a new spot
for his vacation
palace!**

KRONK:
"But, Yzma, I don't want
to visit Europe on vacation!"
YZMA:
"Be quiet
and keep swimming!"

What do you get when you cross
Kronk with a boomerang?
A toy that's too
stupid to return!

What do you do when
Yzma makes a mistake?
Ignore it!

What do you give Yzma
when she's extremely angry?
Anything she wants!

What's worse than
Yzma in a bad mood?
Nothing!

What's mean and scary and
white all over?
**Yzma wearing
cold cream!**

Why doesn't Yzma like
bloodsucking leeches?
Too much competition!

What does Yzma like to eat
on hot summer days?
I scream cones!

KNOCK, KNOCK.
Who's there?
Yzma.
Yzma, who?
Yzma be my lucky day!

11

Why won't Kronk write
with his left hand?
**Because it's the
right thing to do!**

What's the best thing to
call a very angry Kronk?
"Sir."

Why did Kronk throw a clock
out the window?
**He wanted to
see time fly!**

12

How does Kronk do bird impressions?
He eats worms!

What goes *step, step, step,*
"Aaaaaahhh!"?
**Kronk falling
through the trapdoor!**

Why did Kronk bring
Band-Aids to the picnic?
**Because he heard there
would be cold cuts!**

Why does Kronk think
the ocean is friendly?
**Because
it waves.**

What would you call Kuzco if he were brave enough to put his left hand into a pack of jaguars?
"Righty!"

Why did Kuzco cross the road?
Because he felt like it!

What would you call Kuzco if Yzma turned him into a flightless water bird?
An emperor penguin!

Why does Kuzco want to call his new palace Kuzcotopia?
Because ME-topia doesn't sound grand enough!

What would you get if Kuzco had a twin?
Double trouble!

Why did Kuzco
throw a clock
out of the window?
**Because he
felt like it!**

15

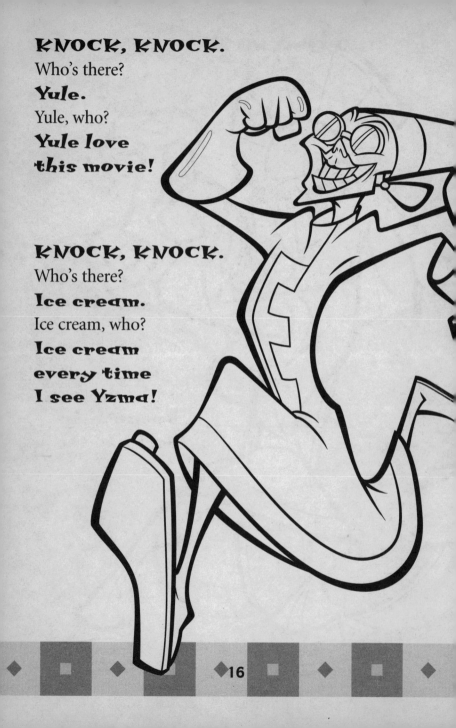

KNOCK, KNOCK.
Who's there?
Yule.
Yule, who?
**Yule love
this movie!**

KNOCK, KNOCK.
Who's there?
Ice cream.
Ice cream, who?
**Ice cream
every time
I see Yzma!**

KRONK:
**"I keep seeing big red spots
in front of my eyes!"**
PACHA:
"Uh-oh. Have you seen a doctor?"
KRONK:
"No. Just big red spots!"

Why did Kronk want to picnic
on the beach?
He wanted a sand-wich!

Why doesn't Kronk like
funny movies?
**He's afraid he'll
laugh his head off!**

Why did Kronk bring sneakers
and shorts on his trip to find Kuzco?
**He heard about
the jungle gym!**

Why did Kronk put
a terrier in the oven?
**Because Yzma said
she wanted a hot dog!**

Why did Kronk put a
terrier in the refrigerator?
**Because Yzma said she wanted
a chili dog!**

Why are llamas big and brown?
**Because if they
were small and gray,
they'd be mice!**

What's brown, pink, and
has four feet?
**A llama sticking
its tongue out!**

How do you make a llama stew?
**Keep it waiting
for hours!**

When does a llama have a trunk?
**When it's going
on vacation!**

How do you keep a llama
from smelling?
Give it a bath!

If Pacha fell into the gorge, what would he fall against? **He'd fall against his will!**

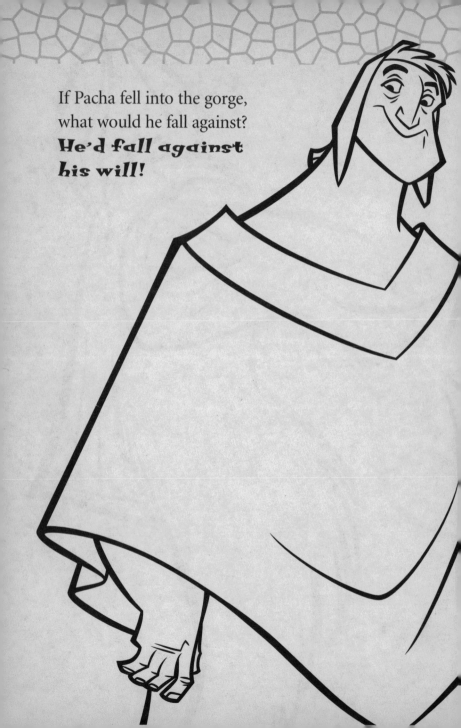

Why doesn't Pacha like Kuzco?
Because he's a royal pain in the neck!

What do you call Pacha after he's been herding llamas in the sun all day?
Red.

What's as big as Pacha, but weighs nothing at all?
His shadow!

Why did Pacha bring an orange to the jungle?
Because the banana split!

What time is it when five guards
chase Kuzco and Pacha?
Five after two!

What time is it when ten
jaguars chase Kuzco?
Ten after one!

What did Kuzco really dislike
about being a llama?
None of his clothes fit!

What happened to Kuzco when he
walked through the screen door?
He strained himself!

How do you make Kuzco stand?
Steal his throne!

What would you get
if you crossed Kronk
with a parrot?
**Hours of
meaningless
conversation.**

What did Kronk say
about the jungle stream?
**"There's
something
fishy going
on in there!"**

Why did Kronk put a
camera in his mouth?
**He needed a
tooth-pic!**

Who is llama's milk best for?
Baby llamas!

Why is a llama's tail six inches long?
**Because if it were twelve
inches long, it'd be a foot!**

Why are llamas always late?
**Because they can't wear
wristwatches!**

What's invisible and smells like a llama?
A jaguar burp!

What vegetable do you get when a herd
of llamas gallops through your garden?
Squash!

What did Kronk ask the llama?
"Why the long face?"

How does Kuzco end every conversation?
"Have a peasant day!"

Why did Kuzco want to work in a clock factory?
**So he could make faces
all day long!**

What animal would Kuzco like to be on a cold day?
A little otter.

Where is Kuzco's temple?
On his forehead!

What time is it when Kuzco takes your house?
Time to get a new house!

Why was the llama in the
middle of a pack of jaguars?
He got lost!

What would you get if you
crossed Kuzco with a lobster?
A selfish shellfish!

Where would Kuzco go
if he lost his llama tail?
To the re-tail store!

What is Kuzco's favorite state?
Maine.
Why?
**Because its abbreviation
spells his favorite
word: ME!**

33

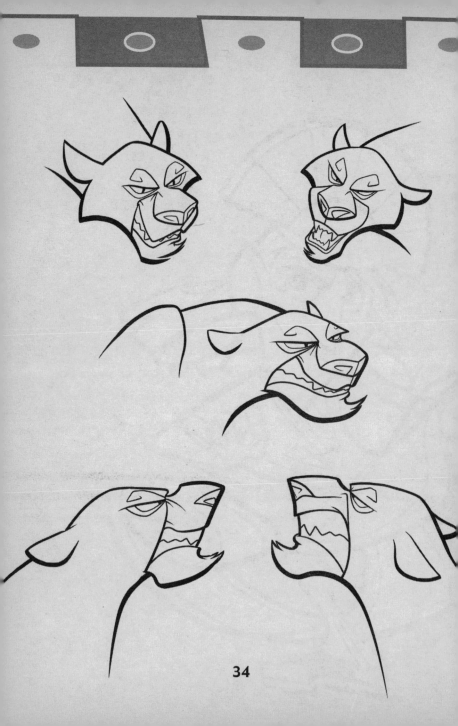

34

What kind of beans do jaguars like?
Human beans!

What did the jaguar mother say when
her son was late for dinner?
**"Sorry, son, everybody's
already been eaten!"**

What do you get if you cross a parrot with a jaguar?
**A creature who talks to you while
gnawing on your arm!**

What do you get if you cross a jaguar with a glove?
**I don't know—but don't stick your
hand in it!**

Why did the jaguar run off the cliff?
He didn't see the ewe turn!

Why was Pacha dizzy?
**Because he'd done too
many good turns!**

If Pacha fell into a jungle river,
what would he become?
Wet!

What's Pacha's favorite
Christmas carol?
"Jungle Bells"!

What kind of umbrella does
Pacha carry when it's raining?
A wet one!

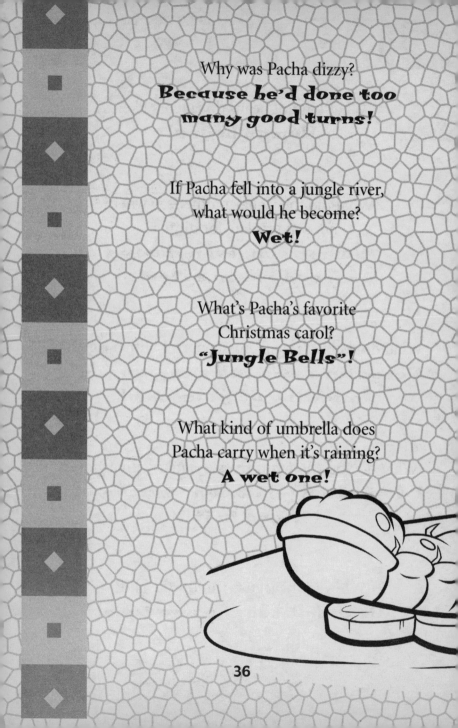

Why did Pacha's dog cross the road?
Because there aren't any chickens in the jungle!

Why can't Pacha tell secrets?
Because llamas carry tails!

What's the difference between
Yzma and a jaguar?
**One's really mean and
cruel, and one's just hungry!**

What should you get Yzma for her birthday?
ANYTHING she wants!

Why did Yzma throw a clock out of the window?
**Because the palace guard was
too heavy!**

What are Yzma's favorite streets?
Dead ends!

KNOCK, KNOCK.

Who's there?

Dozen.

Dozen, who?

**Dozen anyone know
how to help Pacha?**

KNOCK, KNOCK.

Who's there?

Gladys.

Gladys, who?

**Gladys not me who
has to rescue Kuzco!**

KNOCK, KNOCK.

Who's there?

Gopher.

Gopher, who?

**Gopher help—
Yzma's coming!**

Why didn't Kronk bring cookies to bed?
**Because his teddy bear
was stuffed!**

Why did Kronk bring hay to bed?
**Because he wanted to
feed his night-mare!**

Why does Kronk always swim on
his back after lunch?
**Because you're not supposed
to swim on a full stomach!**

Why is Kronk happy that he's not a bird?
**Because he doesn't know
how to fly!**

What has two legs, two arms, a head,
and is very, very dangerous?
Yzma!

How many Yzmas does it take
to change a lightbulb?
**Only one, but she'll change
it into a llama!**

Why did Yzma go out with a fig?
**Because she couldn't
find a date!**

What would you call Yzma
curled up in a ball?
A vicious circle!

Why did Kronk climb the tallest
tree in the jungle?
**Because he thought he was
coming down with something!**

Why did Kronk bring a math book
to the pasture?
**Because he heard they
were going to round up
the llamas!**

Why does Kronk like football?
**Because he thinks a
quarterback is a refund!**

What would happen if Kronk really
spoke his mind?
He'd be speechless!

Why did Kronk try to drive the police car?
**He saw the 911 and thought
it was a Porsche!**

47

What's cute
and cuddly
and bright blue?
**A monkey
holding its breath!**

How do you keep a rattlesnake
from striking?
Pay it decent wages!

How would you describe rain in the jungle?
**Little drops of water falling
from the sky!**

How do you stop a
charging elephant?
**Take away his
credit card!**

How do you send a
message in the jungle?
By moss code!

Why did Kronk bring an
extra shirt to the jungle?
**In case he ran into
Smokey Bare!**

Why did Kronk think that
his bucket was sick?
It was a little pail.

What's the easiest way to confuse Kronk?
**Put him in a round room and
tell him there's a quarter in
the corner!**

Why didn't Kronk look for a job
at a fast-food restaurant?
**Because he thought he was too
tall to be a short-order cook!**

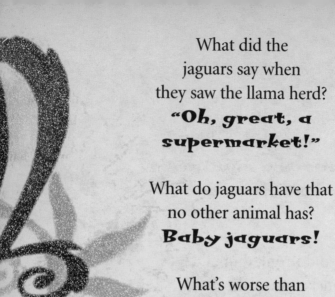

What did the
jaguars say when
they saw the llama herd?
**"Oh, great, a
supermarket!"**

What do jaguars have that
no other animal has?
Baby jaguars!

What's worse than
a hungry jaguar?
An angry Yzma!

52

What would Kuzco do if Yzma
turned him into a tree?
**He wooden open
his mouth!**

What's better than watching
The Emperor's New Groove?
Watching it again!

What did the mother
jaguar say to the baby jaguar
when they saw Kuzco?
**"Dinner
is served."**

What do you get if you
cross Yzma with a skunk?
Very far away!

What do you get if you
cross Yzma with a cat?
**A town with
no mice!**

What do you get when you
cross Yzma with a rose?
**I don't know, but I
wouldn't try to sniff it!**

What did Yzma tell Kronk
to do when he was surrounded
by twelve lions, four giraffes,
and six tigers?
**"Get off the
merry-go-round!"**

Why does Kronk sprinkle
sugar on his pillow every night?
**So he'll have
sweet dreams!**

What do you
get when you
cross Yzma
with a parrot?
**A bird
that gets
a cracker
EVERY time
it asks for
one!**

Why does Yzma say that
she'd be a good judge?
**Because she
thinks she's the
fairest in the land!**

What's the worst part of
The Emperor's New Groove?
When it's over!

Relive the Fun and Adventure with the Movie Soundtrack!

Lyrics by **Sting** • Music by **Sting & David Hartley**
Score Composed by **Mark Shaiman**

WALT DISNEY
THE EMPEROR'S
NEW GROOVE

AN ORIGINAL WALT DISNEY RECORDS SOUNDTRACK

* Artwork subject to change

Features lyrics by Sting,
music by Sting and David Hartley,
score by Marc Shaiman.
Performances by Sting, Tom Jones,
and Eartha Kitt.

Available wherever music is sold.

WALT DISNEY
RECORDS

Look for this exciting title from Disney Interactive

© Disney

WINDOWS 95/98

Over 30 levels of wisecracking gameplay!

www.disneyinteractive.com